SCHOLASTIC

Let's Find Out™

Let's Explore the Five Senses

With City Dog and Country Dog

Laine Falk
Joan Michael

Children's Press®
A Division of Scholastic Inc.
New York Toronto London Auckland Sydney
Mexico City New Delhi Hong Kong
Danbury, Connecticut

Literacy Specialist: Francie Alexander, Chief Academic Officer, Scholastic Inc.

Art Director: Joan Michael

Photographs: all dog photos by James Levin
©Joe Kingleigh/Getty Images (p3 city image); ©Panoramic Images/Getty Images (p3 cows grazing; ©Oote Boe/Alamy (pp4-5 pedestrians); ©Dynamic Graphics/Creatas/Alamy (pp6-7 girl with goat); ©Steve Hamblin/Alamy (pp8-9 Times Square); ©David Ponton/Getty Images (p10-11 path in forest); ©Ambient Images Inc/Alamy (pp12-13 Union Square Market); ©Richard Price/Getty Images (pp14-15 barndyard); ©Photodic via SODA (p15 cow); ©Pixonnet.com/Alamy (pp16-17 hot dog cart); ©Photodisc (p16 hot dog in Charlie's mouth); ©Andrew Hetherington/Getty Images; (pp18-19 field); ©Jules Frazier/Getty Images (p18 water bucket); ©Taylor S. Kennedy/Getty Images (pp20-21 train on stone bridge); ©altrendo nature/Getty Images (pp22-23 outdoor scene); ©Photodisc (p23 soccer ball)

Library of Congress Cataloging-in-Publication Data

Falk, Laine, 1974-
    Let's explore the five senses with city dog and country dog / written by Laine Falk.
        p. cm. — (Let's find out)
    ISBN-13: 978-0-531-14873-0 (lib. bdg.)
    ISBN-10: 0-531-14873-4 (lib. bdg.)
    1. Senses and sensation—Juvenile literature. 2. Dogs—Juvenile
literature. I. Title. II. Series.

QP434.F35 2007
612.8—dc22   2006026333

1 2 3 4 5 6 7 8 9 10 R 16 15 14 13 12 11 10 09 08 07

Charlie

is a city dog.
What does he
see, hear, smell,
taste, and feel
in the city?

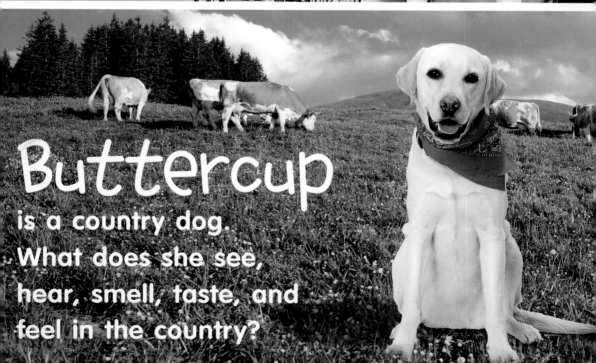

Buttercup

is a country dog.
What does she see,
hear, smell, taste, and
feel in the country?

City Dog

Charlie sees
with his eyes.

Charlie sees crowds of
people in the city.

coming through!

In the country, Buttercup sees something shiny. What does Buttercup see?

Beautiful!

Country Dog
Buttercup sees with her eyes.

Buttercup sees shiny ribbons at the fair in the country.

In the city, Charlie hears something loud.
What does Charlie hear?

City Dog

Charlie hears with his ears.

Charlie hears horns honking in the city.

Beep! Beep! Beep! Beep!

In the country, Buttercup hears something singing. What does Buttercup hear?

Chirp! Chirp!

Chirp! Chirp!

Country Dog
Buttercup
hears with her ears.

Buttercup hears birds singing in the country.

In the city, Charlie smells something sweet.
What does Charlie smell?

Sniff!

City Dog
Charlie smells
with his nose.

Charlie smells flowers at the outdoor market in the city.

Sniff!

In the country, Buttercup smells something fresh. What does Buttercup smell?

Country Dog
Buttercup smells with her nose.

Buttercup smells fresh-cut hay in the country.

In the city, Charlie tastes something yummy. What does Charlie taste?

Chomp!
Chomp!

City Dog

Charlie tastes
with his tongue.

Charlie tastes a juicy hot dog
in the city.

In the country, Buttercup tastes something wet and cold. What does Buttercup taste?

Slurp!

CouNtRy DoG
Buttercup tastes with her tongue.

Buttercup tastes water from a pump in the country.

Slurp!

In the city, Charlie feels something cool.
What does Charlie feel?

BUT WAIT!
Charlie's not in the city!
He's taking a trip
on a train.

City Dog
Charlie feels
with his skin.

He feels the wind on his face
as he rides the train.

Ahhhhh!

Where is he going?

HE'S GOING TO

Country Dog · City Dog

Buttercup and Charlie feel with their paws.

Buttercup feels the soft grass under her paws in the country

SEE BUTTERCUP!

Charlie feels the soft grass under his paws too.

Charlie and Buttercup use their five senses.

They see with their eyes.

They hear with their ears.

They smell with their noses.

They taste with their tongues.

They feel with their skin and paws.

How do you see, hear, smell, taste, and feel?
How did you use your five senses today?